Circles and Curves

by Arthur G. Razzell and K. G. O. Watts

Illustrated by Ellen Raskin

EXPLORING MATHEMATICS SERIES

Donald H. Firl, Educational Consultant

Mathematics Consultant, Rochester, Minnesota Public Schools

Doubleday & Company, Inc.
Garden City, New York

Library of Congress Catalog Card Number

Printed in the United States of America
First Edition in the United States of America

From the earliest times man must have been aware of the roundness of the sun and the moon. At some moment when he cast a stone into water he may have realized that he himself had made the same shape. He has gone on making this shape in many different ways and he has discovered more and more about circles and curves.

You can begin to make discoveries with this experiment. You will need a glass jar like the one below, a juice glass as shown, a penny, and a ball.

Put them one at a time on a gently sloping board and let each one roll down. Did they roll in the same way? Try them in different starting positions. Look carefully at the ways in which they roll.

Next, put the objects one at a time on the sloping board in a position such that they will *not* roll. For instance, the glass jar will not roll in this position.

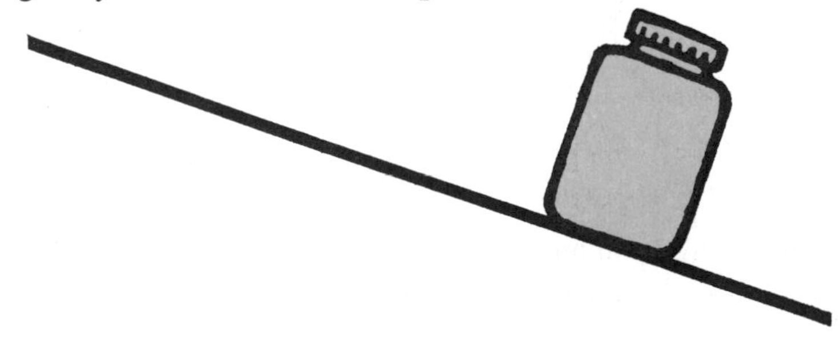

Is one of the objects such that you cannot prevent it from rolling? Think about the reason why each of these objects do roll, and also why one object cannot be prevented from rolling.

Let us look at the objects from different positions.

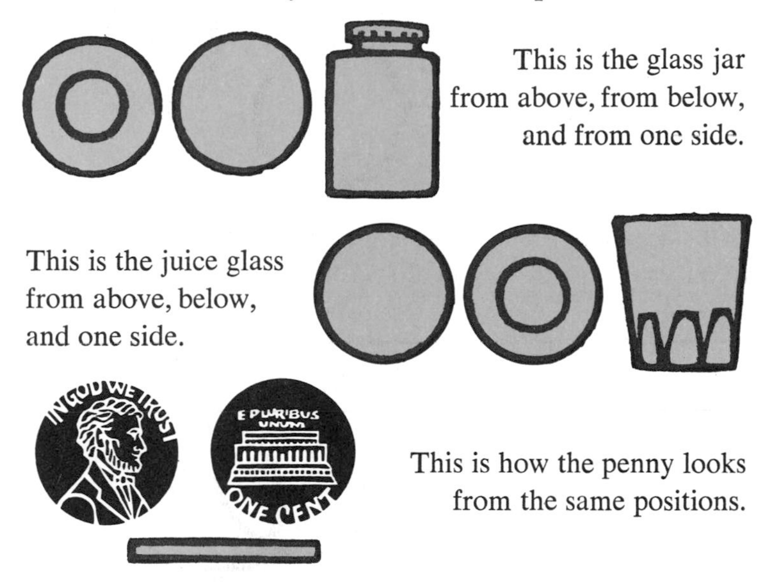

This is the glass jar from above, from below, and from one side.

This is the juice glass from above, below, and one side.

This is how the penny looks from the same positions.

This is the ball from above, from below, and from one side, and from another side, and another, and another!

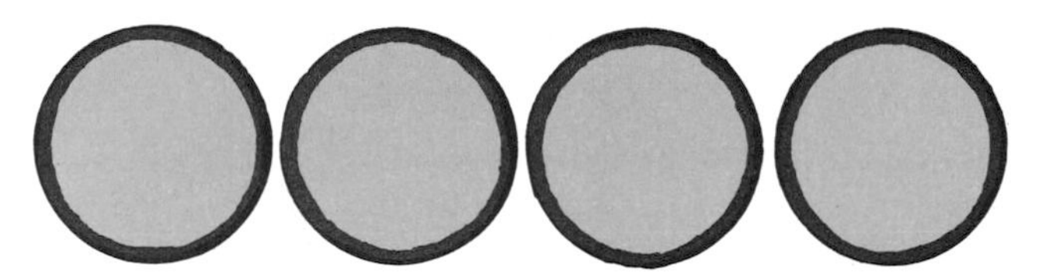

From at least one position all the shapes appear as *circles*; but the ball appears circular from every possible position!

Look around you and make drawings of the circular things you see. Perhaps you could make a *Book of Circles*.

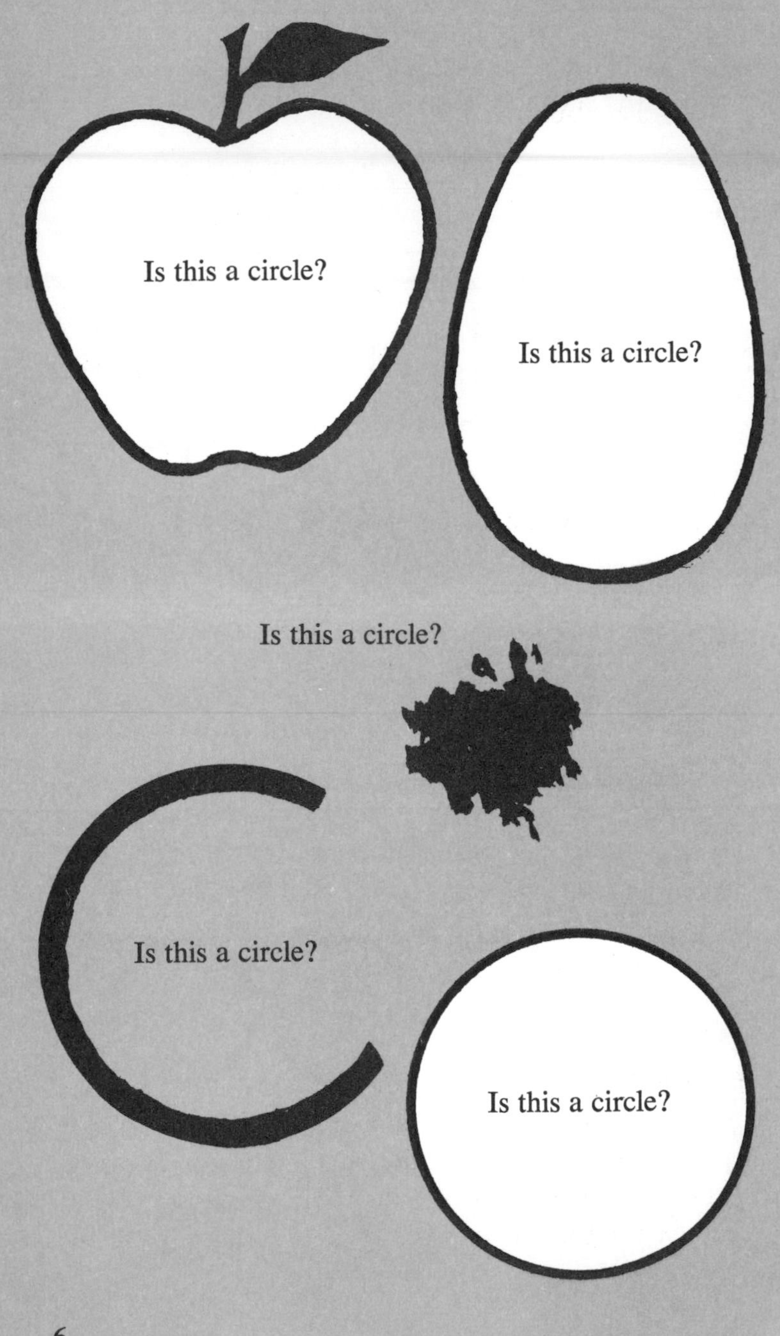
Is this a circle?
Is this a circle?
Is this a circle?
Is this a circle?
Is this a circle?

Only one of the pictures on this page truly makes us think of a circle. What words could be used to describe a circle? We could say "A circle is a curved line."

But this is a curved line, and it does not make a circle.

We could say "A circle is a closed curved line." Yet this is a closed curved line, and it does not make a circle.

We should say "A **circle** is a closed curved line with every point on it exactly the same distance from a point inside called its center." That does describe a circle. One reason why the Ancient Greeks called the circle *The Perfect Curve* is because each point on it is the same distance from the center.

Here are two experiments for you to try. Tie a small weight to a piece of string, loop the end of the string around a finger, and whirl the weight around you. It would be best if you did this out of doors. The path of the weight will be that of a complete circle if you whirl it fast enough.

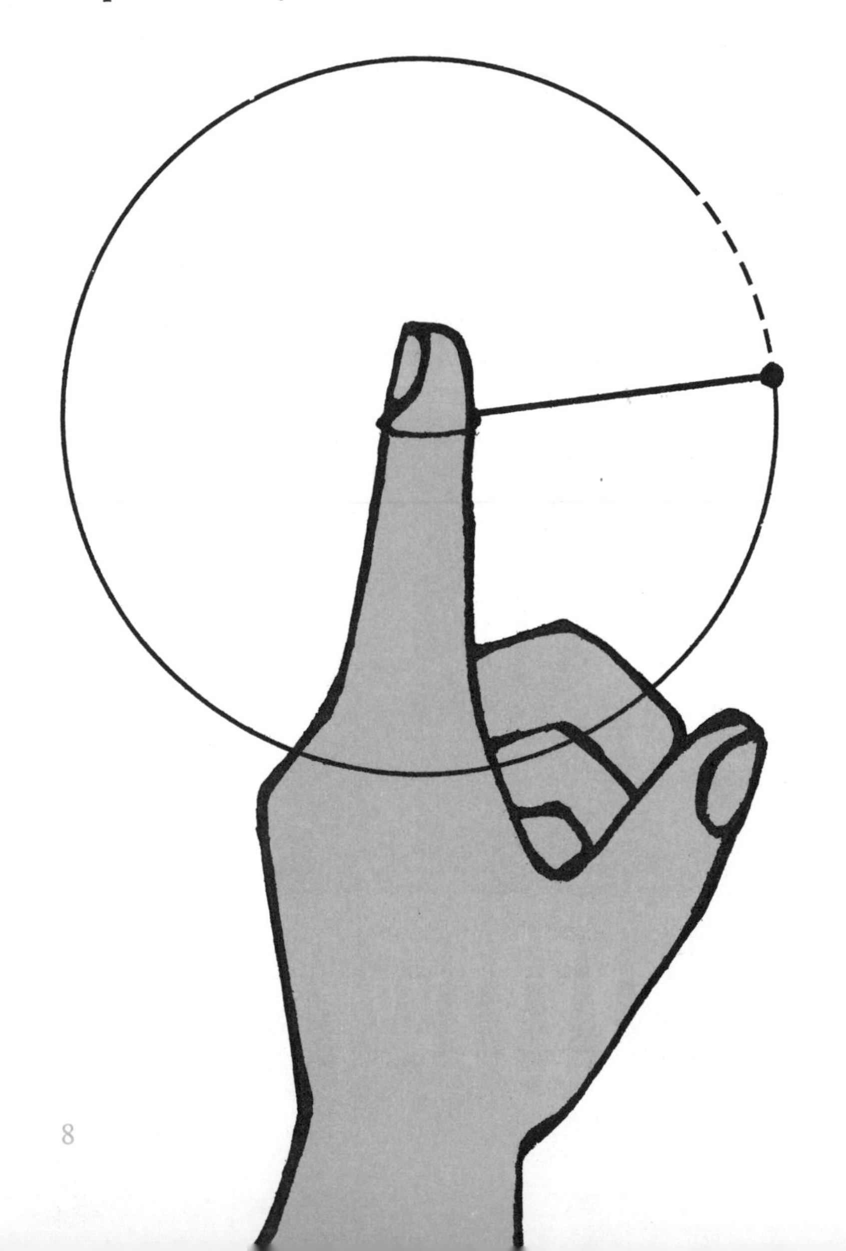

The second experiment is started by putting a pin or a thumb tack into a board. Then take a long loop of thread and drop it over the pin or tack. Place a pencil point in the other end of the loop. Pull the pencil around the pin (or tack) evenly, letting the tightness of the thread guide its path.

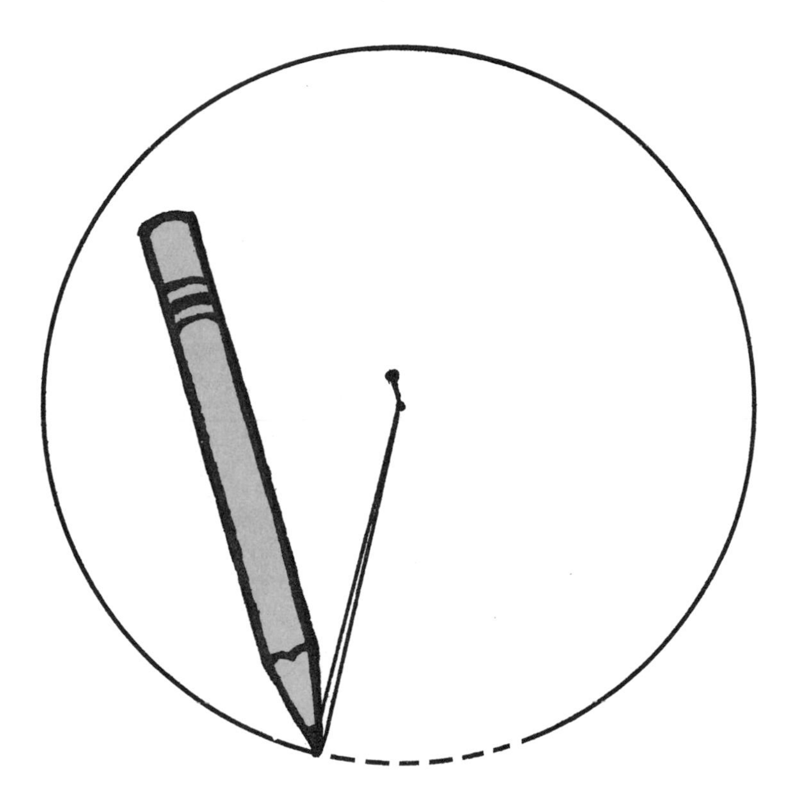

Here is the description of a circle again:

A circle is a closed line with every point on it exactly the same distance from a point inside called its center.

Can you see why the two experiments produced circles?

Map

We know the Greeks and Romans were interested in studying the circle, and all of the names of its parts come from either Greek or Latin words.

Center comes from a Greek word "kentron," which means "a sharp point." The center is the middle point of the inside of a circle.

Circumference comes from two Latin words: "circum" meaning "round," and "ferre" meaning "to carry." The circumference is the length of the circle–or as some may say, "the distance around the circle."

Diameter comes from two Greek words: "dia" meaning "through," and "metron" meaning "a measure." The diameter is the distance between any two "opposite" points on the circle, measured along a straight line through the center.

Radius is a Latin word meaning "spoke of a wheel." If you imagine a number of these drawn for a circle you will soon think of a wagon wheel. If one wishes to talk about more than one radius, he must say "radii" just as the Romans did. A radius is the straight path from any point on the circle to the center of the circle.

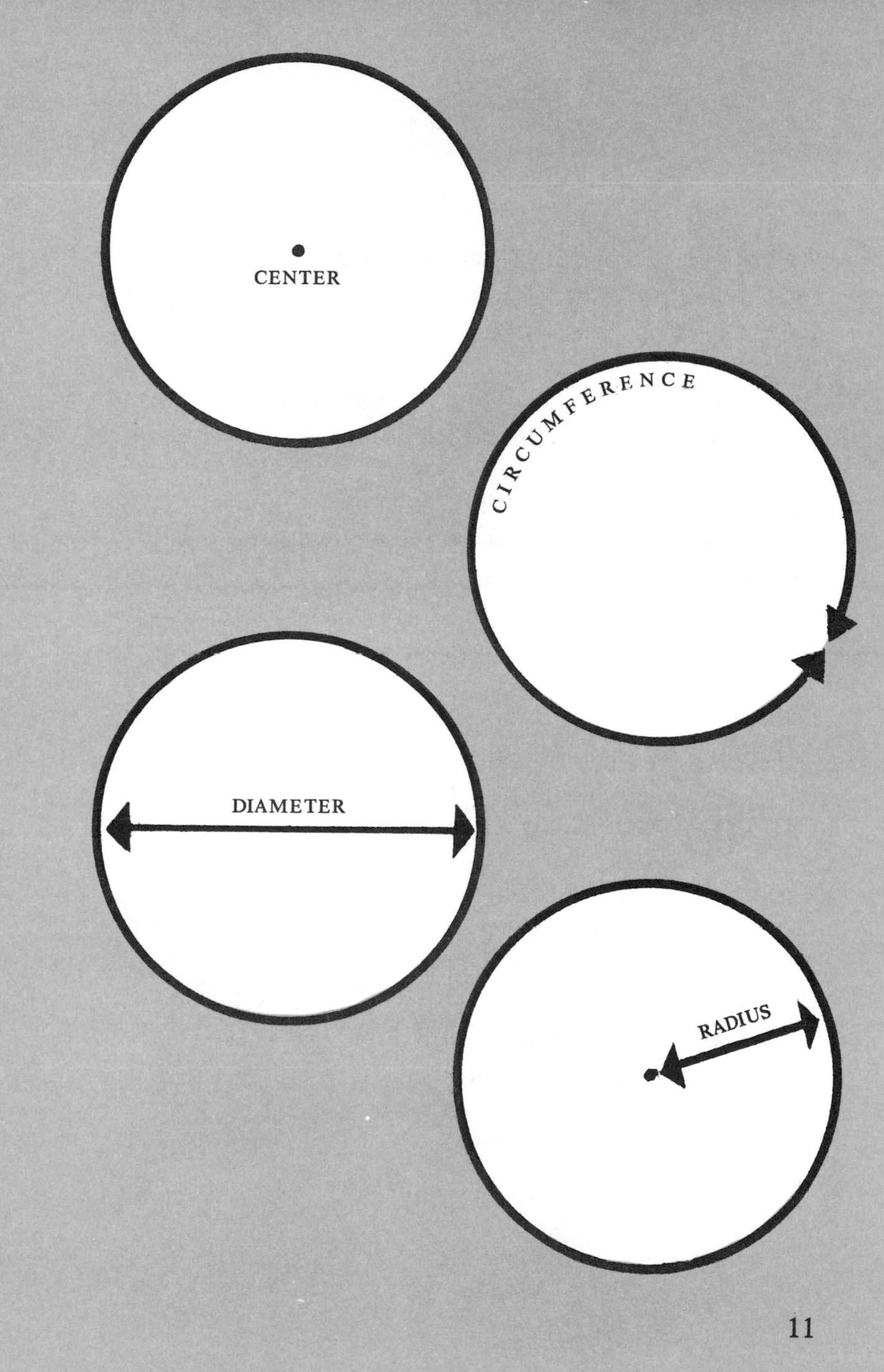
CENTER
CIRCUMFERENCE
DIAMETER
RADIUS

Before mathematicians really began to study the circle carefully, it had already been put to some practical uses in the form of a wheel. The potter had found that it helped him to make better pots and jars. Wagons and chariots moved on wheels made in various ways.

As time went on men found more and more ways to make wheels and how to use them for different purposes. They invented the water wheel with its paddles and cog wheels with interlocking teeth for machinery.

In the Old Testament we can read about the great bronze basin that stood in the courtyard of Solomon's Temple. "...He made a molten sea, ten cubits from one brim to the other; it was round all about...A line of thirty cubits did compass it round...."

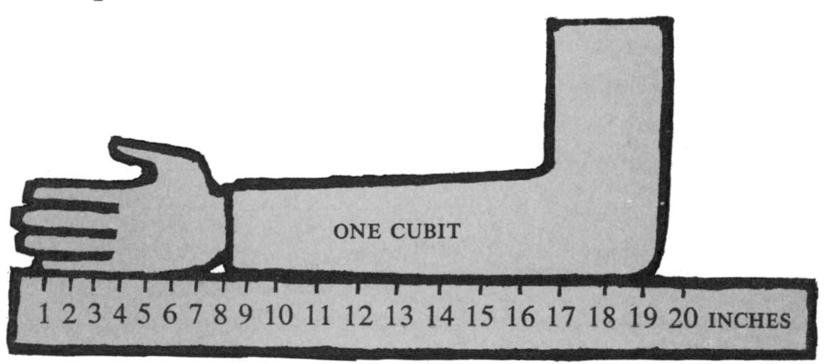

This tells us that in those days men thought the circumference of a circle was three times as long as its diameter. Later the Greeks found it was more than three times the diameter. In fact, Archimedes, a Greek mathematician who lived 2,000 years ago, said it was 3-1/7 times the length of the diameter.

You can try an experiment to see if he was right.

Place two blocks of wood on a sheet of newspaper folded in half. Carefully line up the edges of the blocks with folded edge of the paper. Then stand a salt box between the blocks and slide them together until they touch each side. Measure the distance between the blocks and you have found the diameter of the box.

Next wrap a long narrow strip of paper tightly around the box and stick a pin through the overlapping ends into the box. Unroll the paper strip and measure the distance between the holes; this distance will be the circumference of the salt box.

Divide the diameter of the salt box into its circumference. The measurements will have to be made very, very carefully, recording the smallest fraction of an inch. If you have done the measuring carefully, then your answer to the division will be a little more than three. If you used fractions in doing the division, the answer should be about 3-1/7. If you have used decimals, then it should be about 3.14. If your measurements were absolutely accurate, the answer would be 3.141592... and then perhaps you would give up. The number can't be completed.

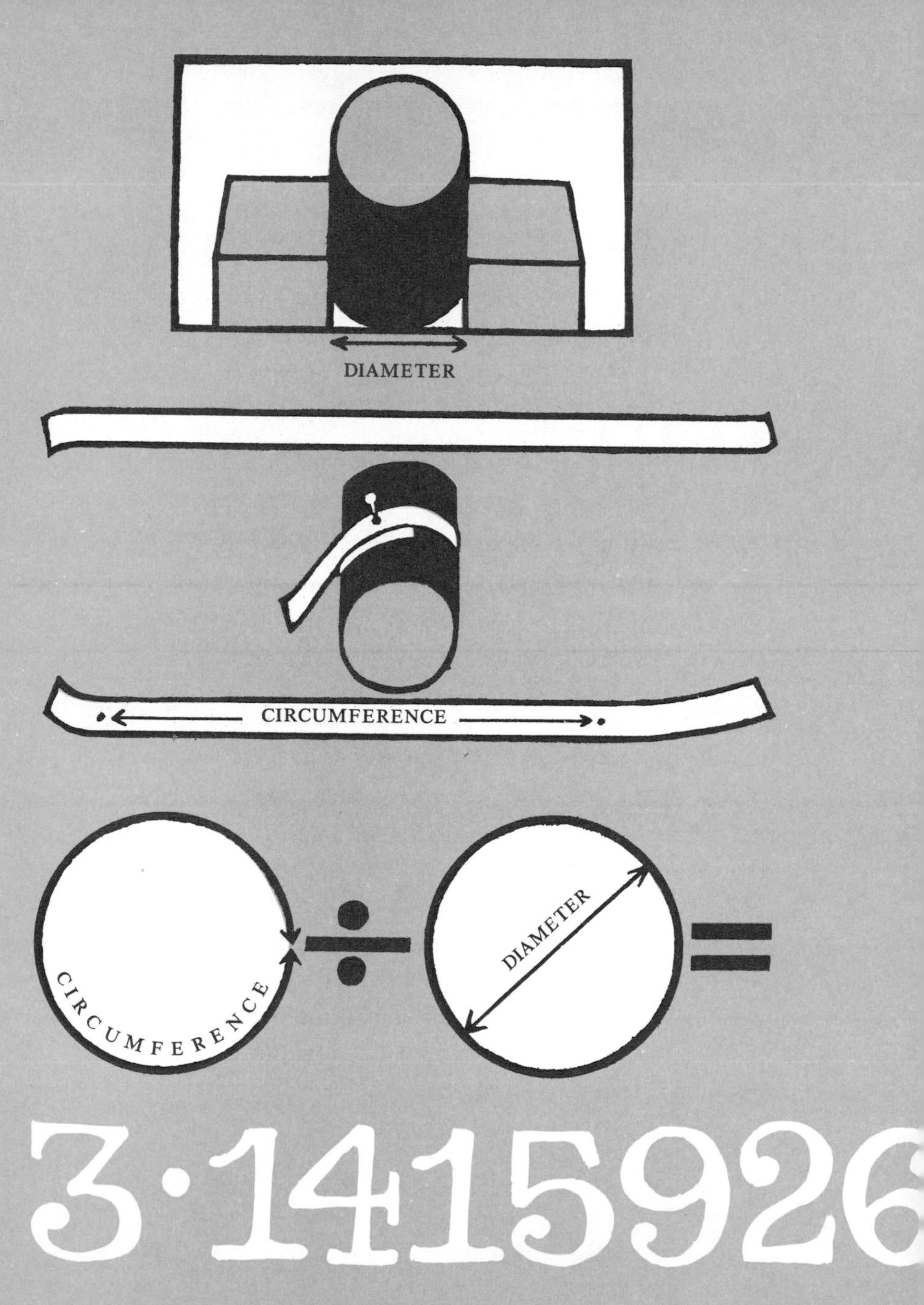
DIAMETER
CIRCUMFERENCE
CIRCUMFERENCE
DIAMETER
3·1415926

In the sixteenth century a German named Ludolf von Ceulen carried on the division until he had completed 35 decimal places. 3.14159265358979323846264338327950288 . . . If you were a German school child, you might be taught that the name for this number is the Ludolfian Number. We use a Greek letter to stand for it, π, which is called **pi**. (For most of our calculations we use the number 3.1416, or even 3.14.) When Ludolf died, the number he had found was carved on his tombstone.

In modern times the number π has been worked out to 10,000 decimal places on a computer; but the number still is not completed. If you find it hard to remember that π is 3.1416 to four decimal places; then this sentence may help you:

YES, I HAVE A NUMBER
3 . 1 4 1 6

The number of letters in each word gives you the help you need. If you like, you can make up your own sentence. For instance:

MOM, I MADE A CIRCLE
3 1 4 1 6

does the same job.

535897932

Here is an unusual way to make a circle. Fold a piece of plain paper like this to form a right angle (square corner) at the place marked R.

Put two pins (or thumb tacks) through the piece of paper in a board about 1½ inches apart. Push the right angle marked R up between the pins or tacks so that the sides of the folded paper touch them. Make a dot on the paper at the place where R touches it. Change the position many times, like this:

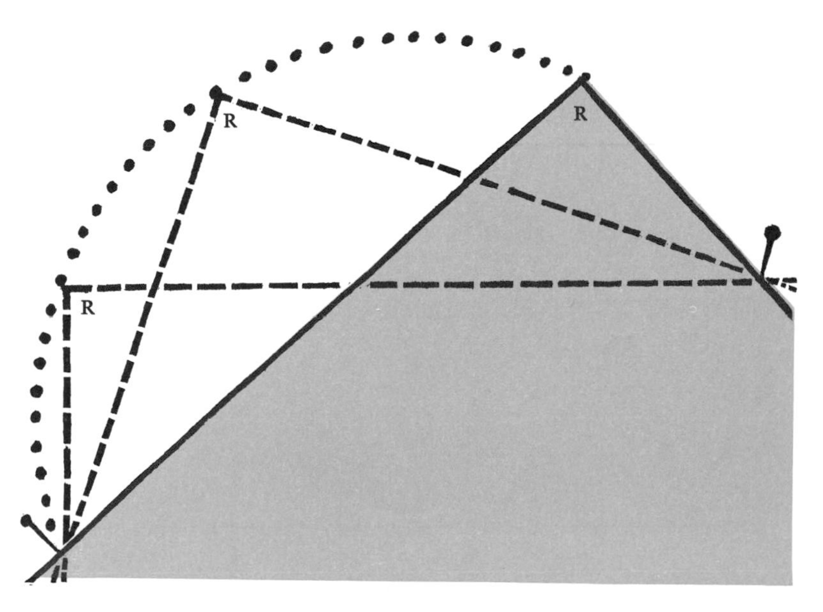

Smoothly connect the dots. You will have drawn half a circle. This is called a **semicircle** (the Latin word "semi" means "half"). If you put your right angle down between the pins and repeat the pattern you will draw the other semi-circle that will complete the whole circle.

A
B
2″
1
2
2″

Here is another way to make a circle. Take a strip of thin cardboard 5 inches long and 2 inches wide. Mark it like this and cut along the dotted line. Again put two pins or tacks in a board about 1½ inches apart. Draw a straight line between them. Place the piece marked 1 up between the pins, touching both of them. Make a dot where the point A touches the paper. Change the position of A, making sure the paper is still touching the pins. Then make another dot. Do this many times until you have enough dots to connect with a smooth curve. Remove part 1, and push part 2 *down* between the pins and mark dots in the same way where the point B touches the paper.

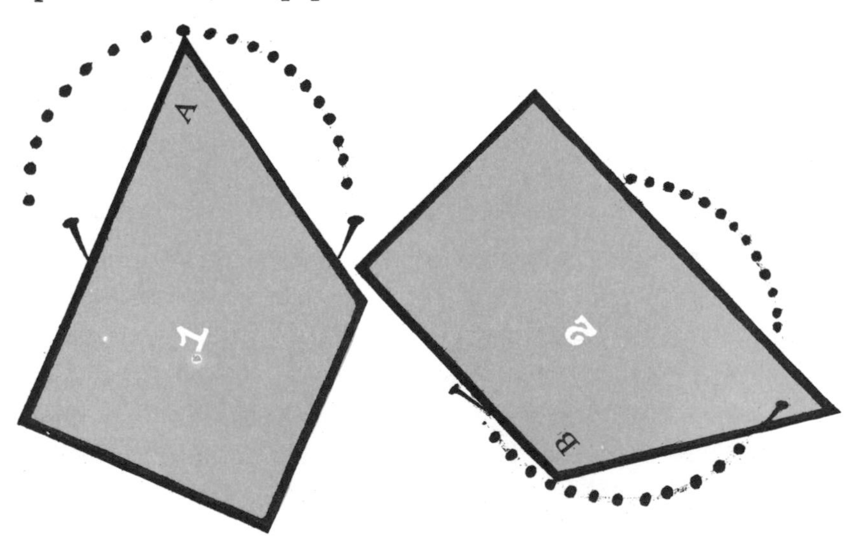

Join all of the dots smoothly and you will have made a circle like this:

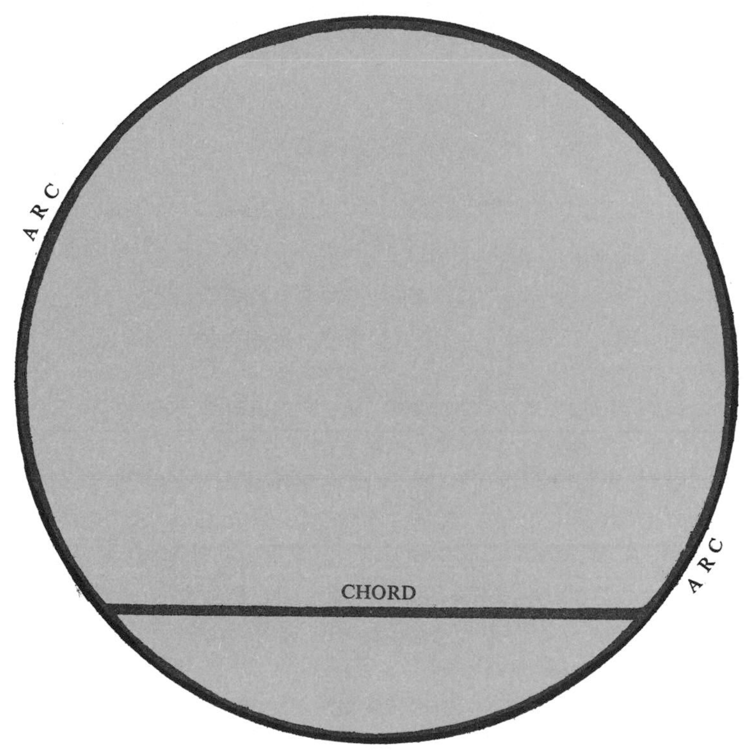

The straight line is called a **chord;** and each curved line you made is called an **arc.** Chord comes from a Latin word meaning "string."

A chord is any straight line drawn from one point on a circle to another point on the circle. A diameter is a special chord. Arc is from a Latin word that means "bow." An arc is any part of a circle that is less than the whole circle. A semicircle is a very special arc. If you will turn your book sideways, you will see that one of the arcs will make a very good "bow" for the "string."

Suppose you were a gold prospector in the days of the Great Gold Rush. When you went to file your claim, the sheriff showed you this notice:

YUKON TERRITORY

CLAIMS REGULATIONS.

NO SINGLE CLAIM SHALL MEASURE

MORE THAN 22 YARDS

AROUND ITS BOUNDARY

What shape would your land claim have to be if you are to get the largest possible digging space?

You can experiment by using a piece of string. This can stand for your 22 yard boundary. Tie the string to make a closed piece 22 inches long. Then lay it on a piece of paper marked off into one-inch squares. Count the number of squares inside the boundary made by the string to measure the area inside. Make new shapes and count the squares inside each time. Do this until you have discovered the shape that will have the most squares in it. It will be the one you would use for your claim.

Here are some suggestions to start you off. ▶

Now try a pentagon or a hexagon; then a circle. You will find it harder to count squares accurately with these shapes. Even though you cannot count the squares accurately, which shape *seems* to have the largest area? How many squares do you estimate are inside the circle?

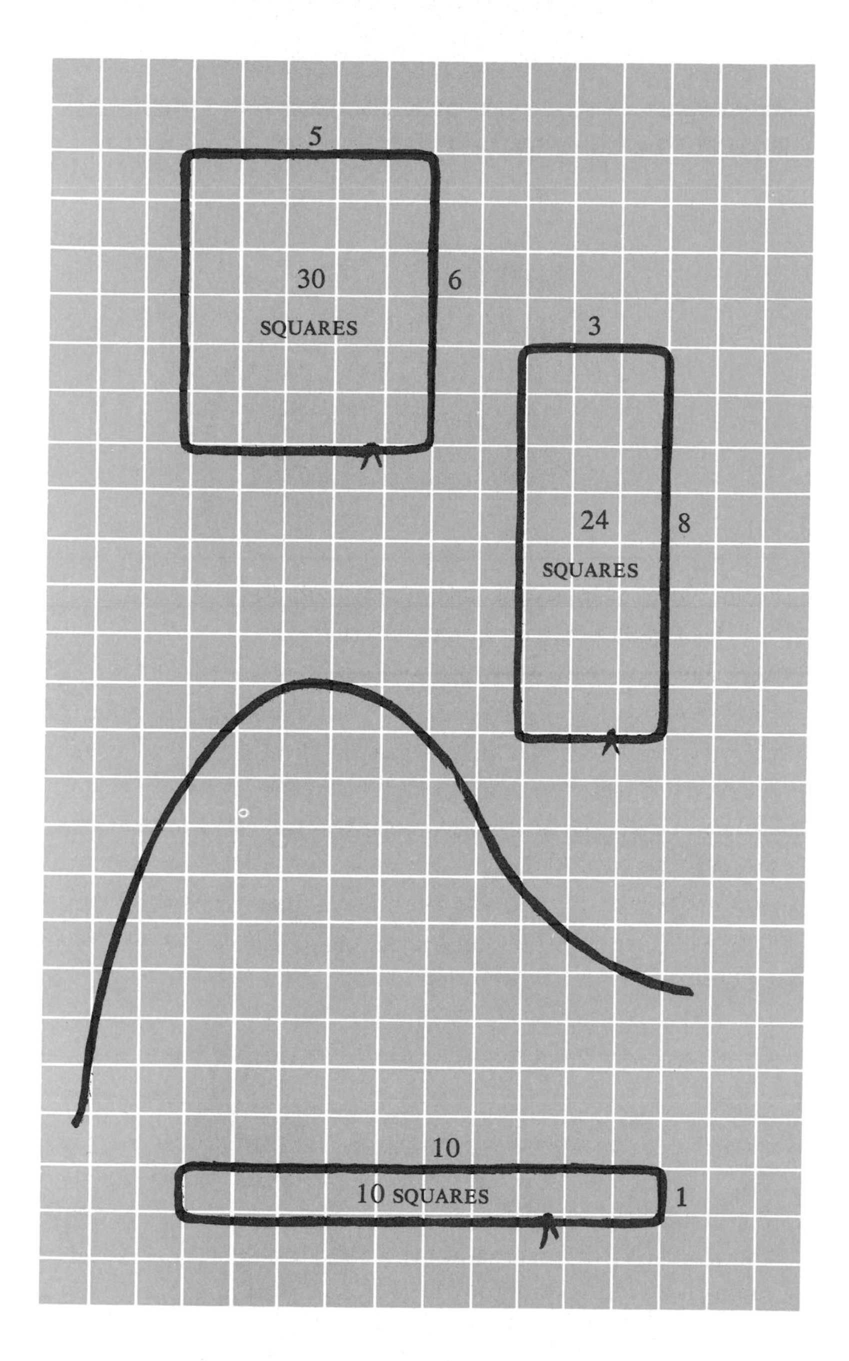
5
30
SQUARES
6
3
24
SQUARES
8
10
10 SQUARES
1

There is another way to find the area of a circle: instead of counting squares, we can use π. Take some sturdy paper or thin cardboard and using the right angle method on page 13 cut out a circle 2 inches in radius. Fold the circle in half and color one half.

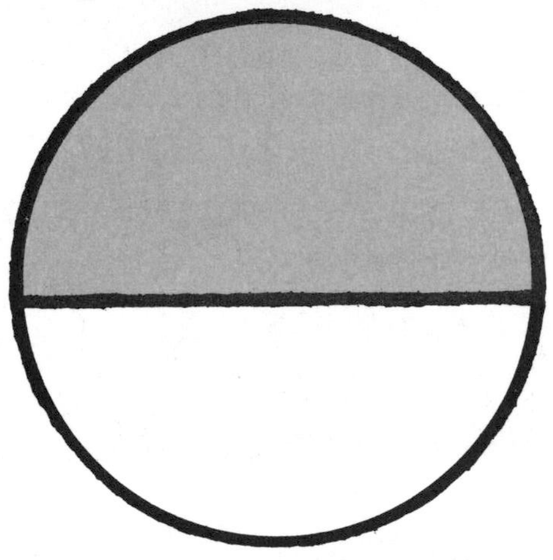

Now fold the circle into fourths, then into eighths. Open it out and cut along the folds; then arrange the eight pieces like this:

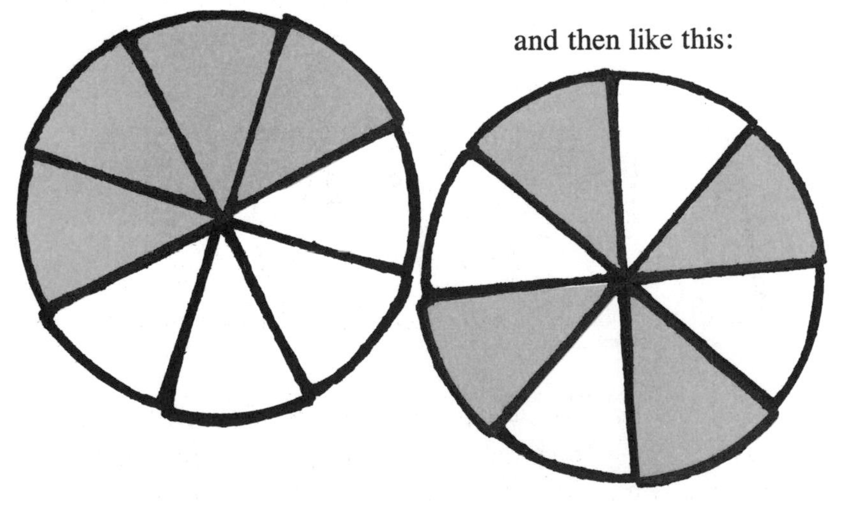

and then like this:

In both cases you can see that the curved edges of the colored pieces make up half the circumference in length. Now re-arrange the pieces like this to form a rough rectangle in shape. The short side of the rectangle is equal in length to the radius of the circle, which is 2 inches. The other side of the rectangle is equal in length to half the circumference of the circle, which is about 6¼ inches.

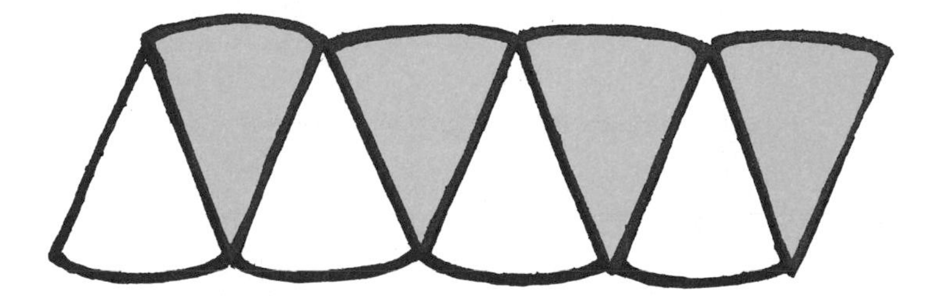

If you now cut each of the eight sections in half and arrange them like this you will see that the shape is nearer that of a true rectangle. The short side is still 2 inches and the long side is still half the circumference (but it is nearer to being a straight line).

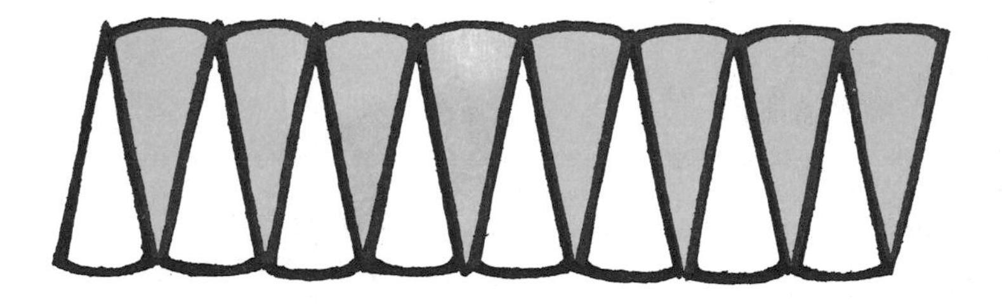

If you are very careful, you may be able to cut each of the 16 pieces in half once more. You could paste the pieces down on another piece of paper to keep them from slipping.

Here is a drawing of the 32 pieces. It shows that the more pieces one makes the straighter the long side becomes. Do you see how the corners also become more like right angles?

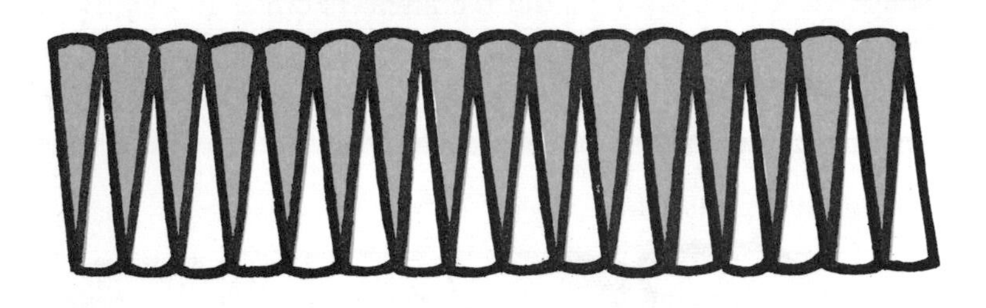

We know the circumference of a circle is equal to its diameter multiplied by π. This is the same thing as twice the radius times π. So half of the circumference will be just one radius times π. We can write this as r x π. We now have found another way of describing the length of the long side of our "rectangle" made from a circle. It is r x π.

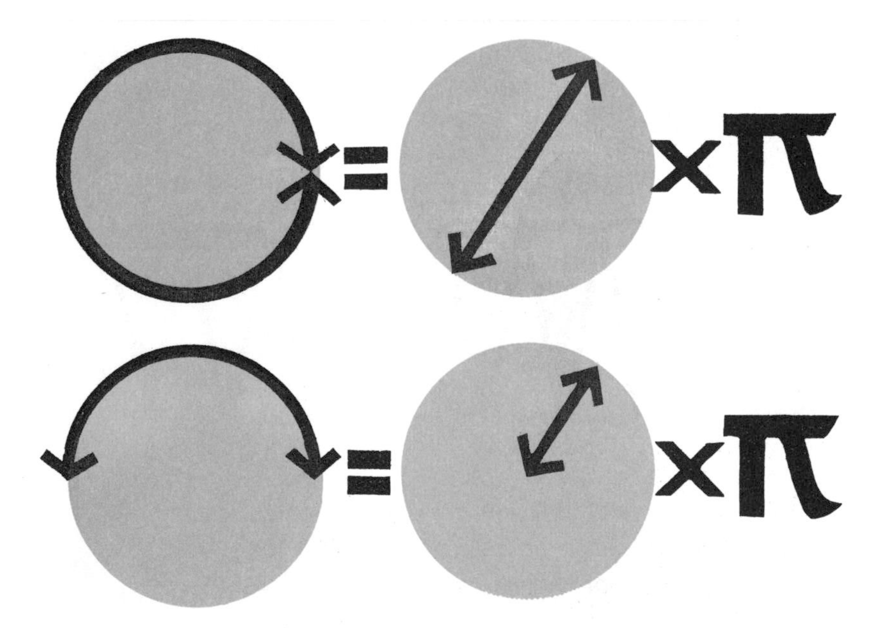

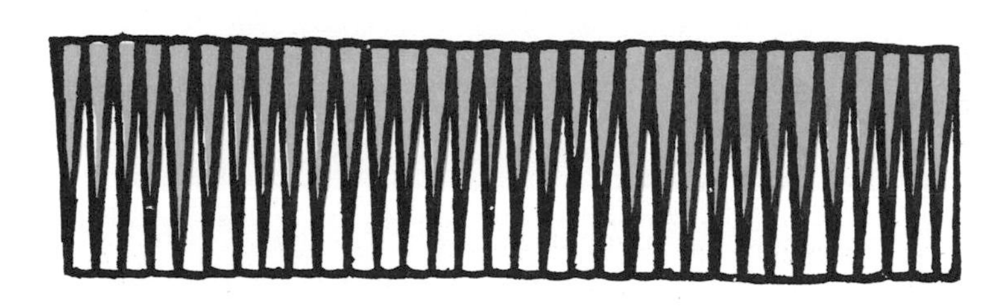

This next drawing shows a "rectangle" made from a circle cut into 64 parts. You can see that its shape is very nearly an actual rectangle. The long side will measure r x π and its height is r. We can find the area of the rectangle by multiplying the measures of the two sides together, or r by r x π. The product is usually written as πr^2. The area of the circle will of course be the same. Thus we have found that the area of a circle can be found from the length of its radius by using πr^2.

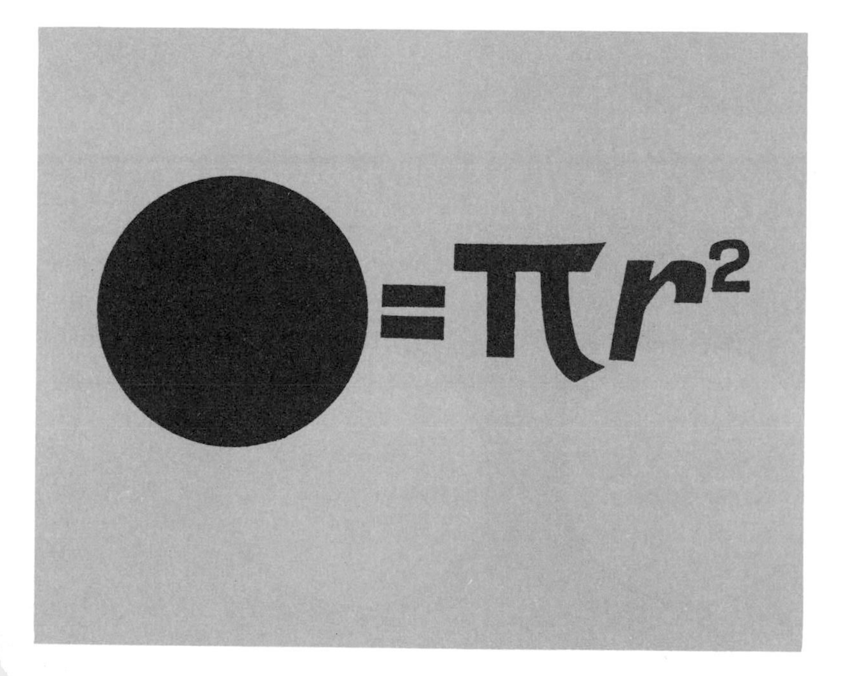

You have read about the circumference of a circle several times in this book. Here are two puzzles that are concerned with it.

Here is a penny. How many other pennies could be fitted around it? Each penny is to touch its neighbor and the middle penny. Think about this puzzle before you do it.

You did not have to be very rich to do that one. The next puzzle needs even less money. Place two pennies like this, with the word "We" from "In God We Trust" touching at the beginning of a line. Roll the top penny carefully along the line until it has made one complete turn. Mark this point on the line. Do the same with the other penny under the line. "We" should touch the first mark.

Now put the pennies back again in the same positions. If you roll the top penny around the edge of the lower penny until the words "We" are together again, how many complete turns will it take? Think about it. Remember what happened in the first part of the puzzle. Now do it, but be sure to hold the lower penny still and do not let the top one slip as it turns. This works better with two dimes or two quarters, because the grooved edges will grip, but they are not so easy to come by!

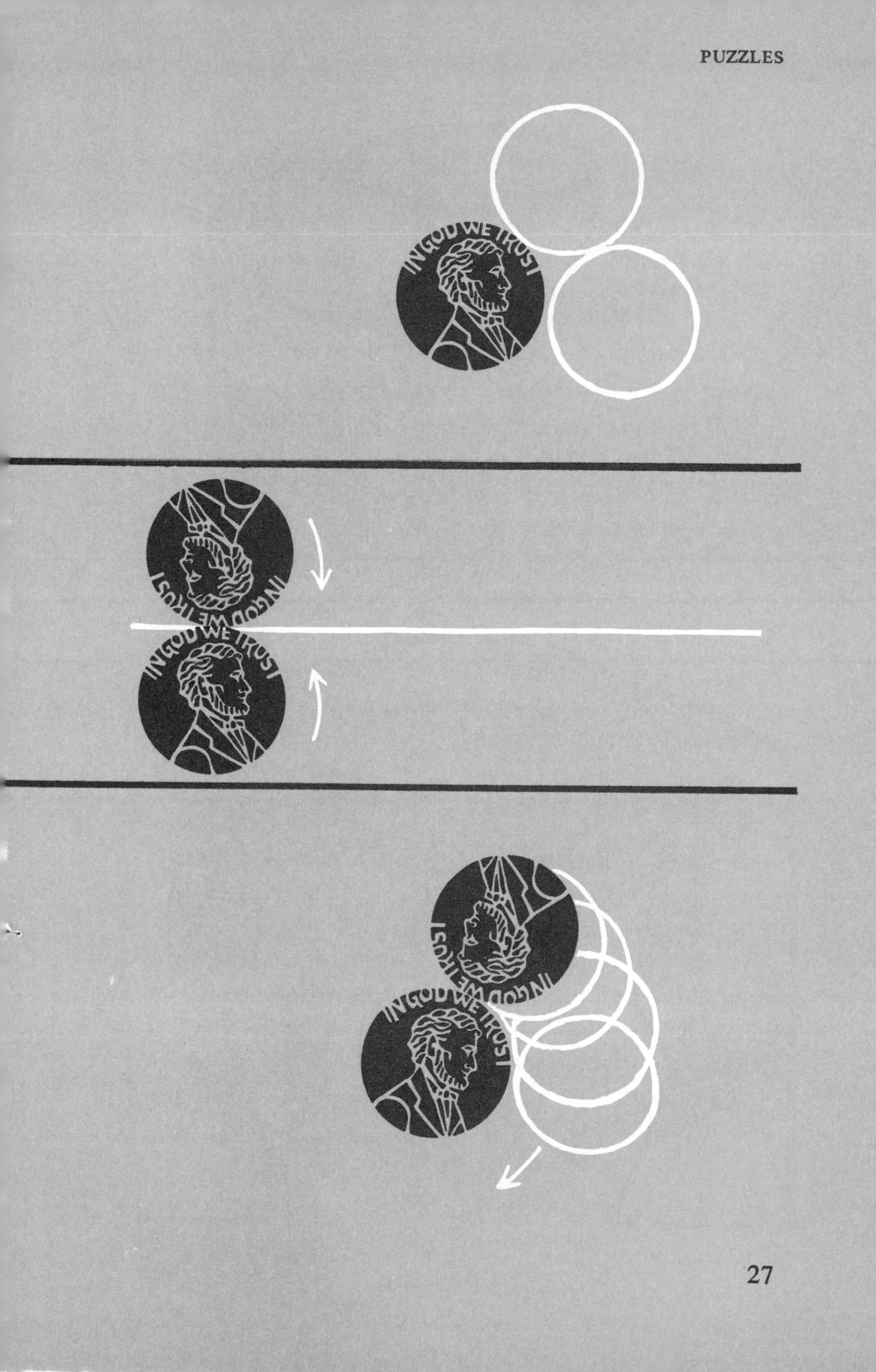
IN GOD WE TRUST

The cup and saucer in this picture are actually circular, but in this view they appear to have a different shape. It is called an **ellipse.** You can see it forming as you rotate a plate or lid between your fingers. Notice how your fingers stay the same distance apart all of the time; it is only the vertical distance that seems to change.

Make a circle 3 inches in diameter. Draw lines a quarter of an inch apart at right angles to the diameter. Mark the middle point between the diameter and the circle on each one. Then join these points with a smooth curving line. You will have made an ellipse. Another ellipse can be made by marking quarter distances from the diameter to the circle.

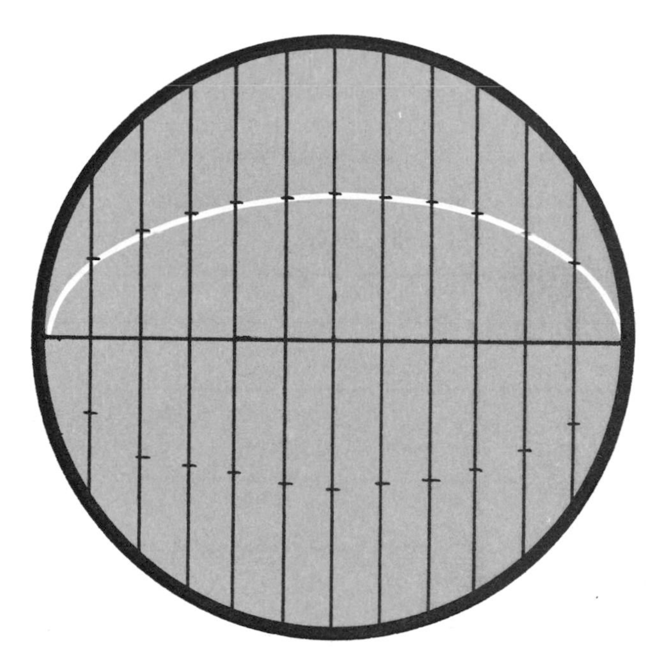

These ellipses are related to the circle in the same way as those you saw when you rotated the plate or lid in your fingers.

A circle is drawn around *one* point called its center. An ellipse is drawn using *two* points. Each point is called a **focus.** For more than one we say focuses. Focus is a Latin word which means "hearth."

Stick two pins or tacks 2 inches apart in a pine board. Drop a loop of thread about 6 inches long over them both. Put your pencil point in the loop and draw it around the pins or tacks, keeping the thread tight like this:

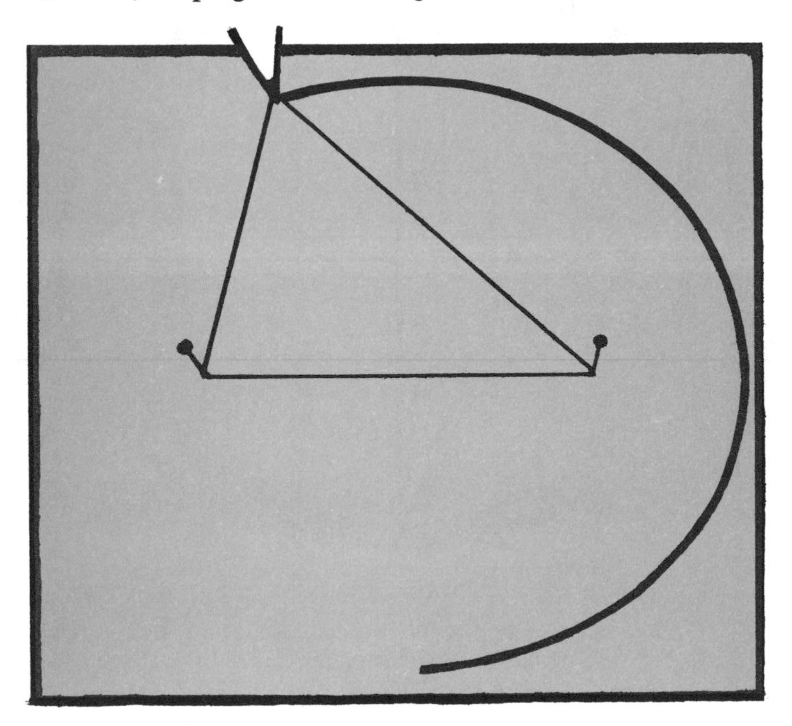

If you find the midpoint of this axis and draw another line at right angles to the first one until it meets the ellipse again, you will have drawn the **minor axis** of the ellipse. Which axis did your fingers touch when you rotated the plate or lid to make an ellipse?

Each pin or tack is a focus of the ellipse you have drawn. Take the pins or tacks out and connect the two holes with a straight line. Extend this line in each direction until it meets the curve. This line, which passes through the two foci of the ellipse, is called the **major axis** of the ellipse.

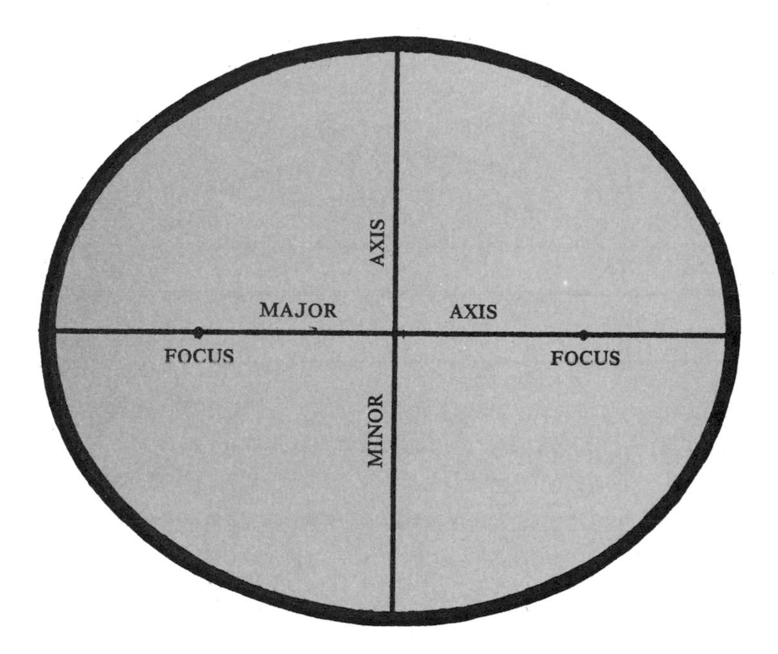

It is easy to find circles in the things around you, but ellipses are not quite so plentiful. You may find one in the shape of a platter or in a transistor radio part.

Although we do not see it so often, the ellipse is still an important curve. In fact, it is perhaps the most important and exciting curve of all. The artificial satellites that men have sent out into space each have a path that is an ellipse, too.

There are many curves in nature that are easily traced, or made without effort.

> The way that a skier sails through the air as he leaps from a snow mound...
> The path that a ball takes as it is thrown from one person to another...
> The fall of water from a fountain in a park...

All these curves are called **parabolas.**

The parabola gets part of its name from a Greek word meaning "thrown." Any object which is thrown, shot, or propelled into the atmosphere follows this curve as it is pulled by the force of gravity. The mathematician draws this curve on special squared-off paper using special calculation. You can do it more simply by just drawing straight lines.

Draw two straight lines at right angles to each other. Make each about 6 inches long and mark them at ¼ inch intervals.

Label the marks with numbers as in this drawing. With a straight line connect the pairs of like numbers, 1 to 1, 2 to 2, 3 to 3, and so on. As you do this you will see a parabola gradually forming.

You will want to try again with the numbered lines (axes) at an angle greater than a right angle and then again with the angle less than a right angle.

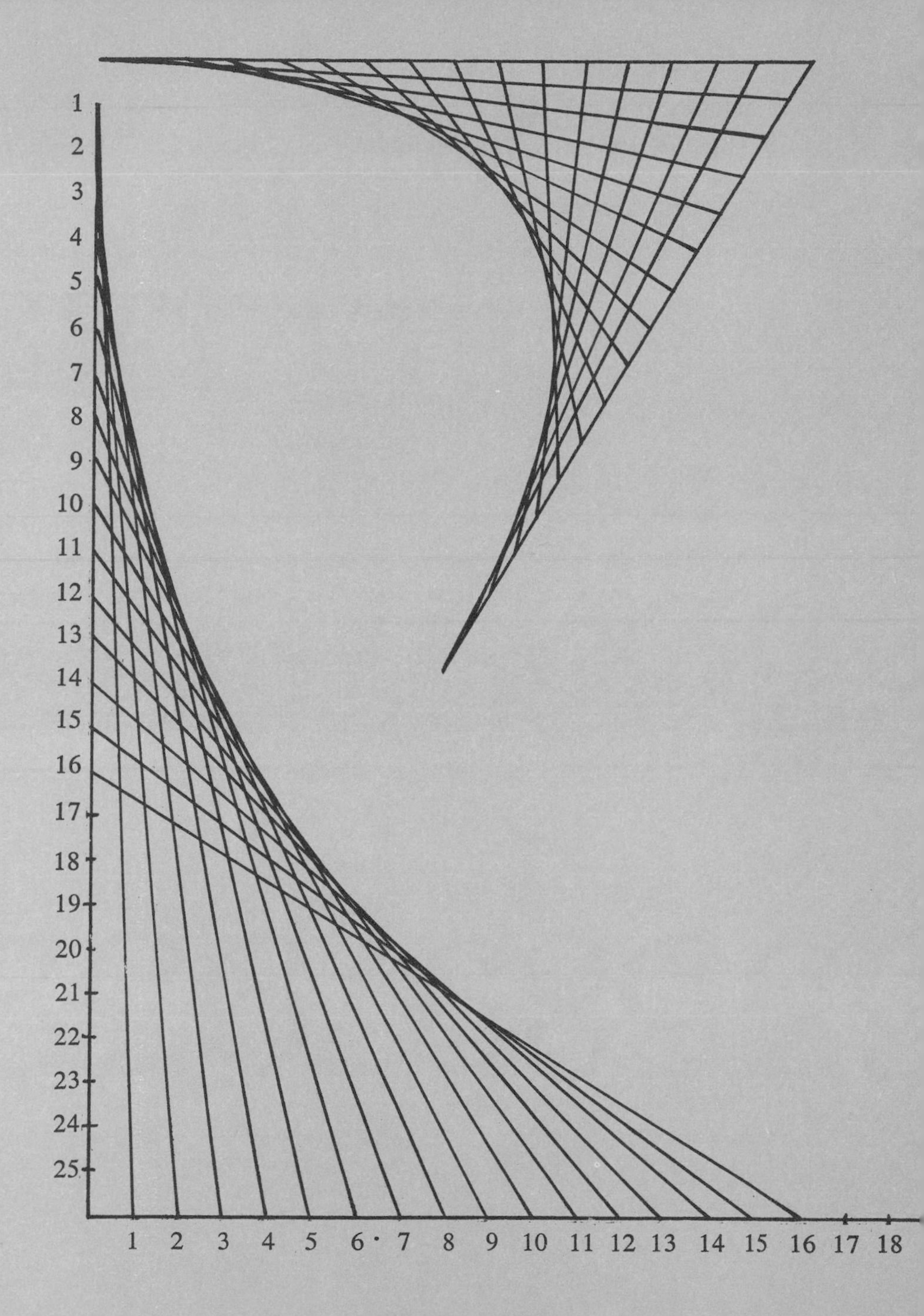
1
2
3
4
5
6
7
8
9
10
11
12
13
14
15
16
17
18
19
20
21
22
23
24
25
1 2 3 4 5 6 7 8 9 10 11 12 13 14 15 16 17 18

The polished reflector of a searchlight and the rotating bowl of a radar detection device are both parabolic. This shape has special ways of collecting and reflecting light waves, sound waves, and electromagnetic waves. It is often used in scientific work.

You can see a parabola formed (as well as a circle and an ellipse) by doing this experiment. Take a flashlight and turn the beam straight onto a piece of paper.

Notice the shape of the patch of light.

Now tilt the flashlight a little. The patch changes to this shape.

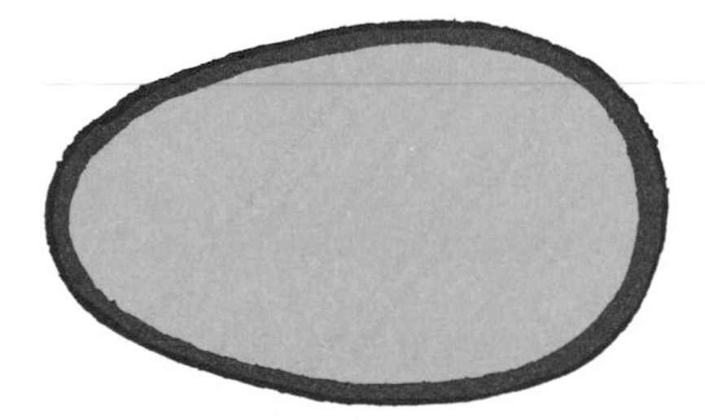

Tilt the flashlight a litle more. The patch is now in the shape of a parabola.

The shells of certain wet-life creatures, such as the snail, the whelk, the periwinkle, and the chambered nautilus, show a **spiral** method of animal growth and development. The fossil remains of the prehistoric ammonite are also like this.

If you have watched the pattern water makes as it disappears down the drain of your bath then you have seen a spiral. Its name is from a Greek word meaning "coil." Spirals are also found in other places where you can look at them longer. You may wish to make a collection of examples of spirals and make a record of where you found them.

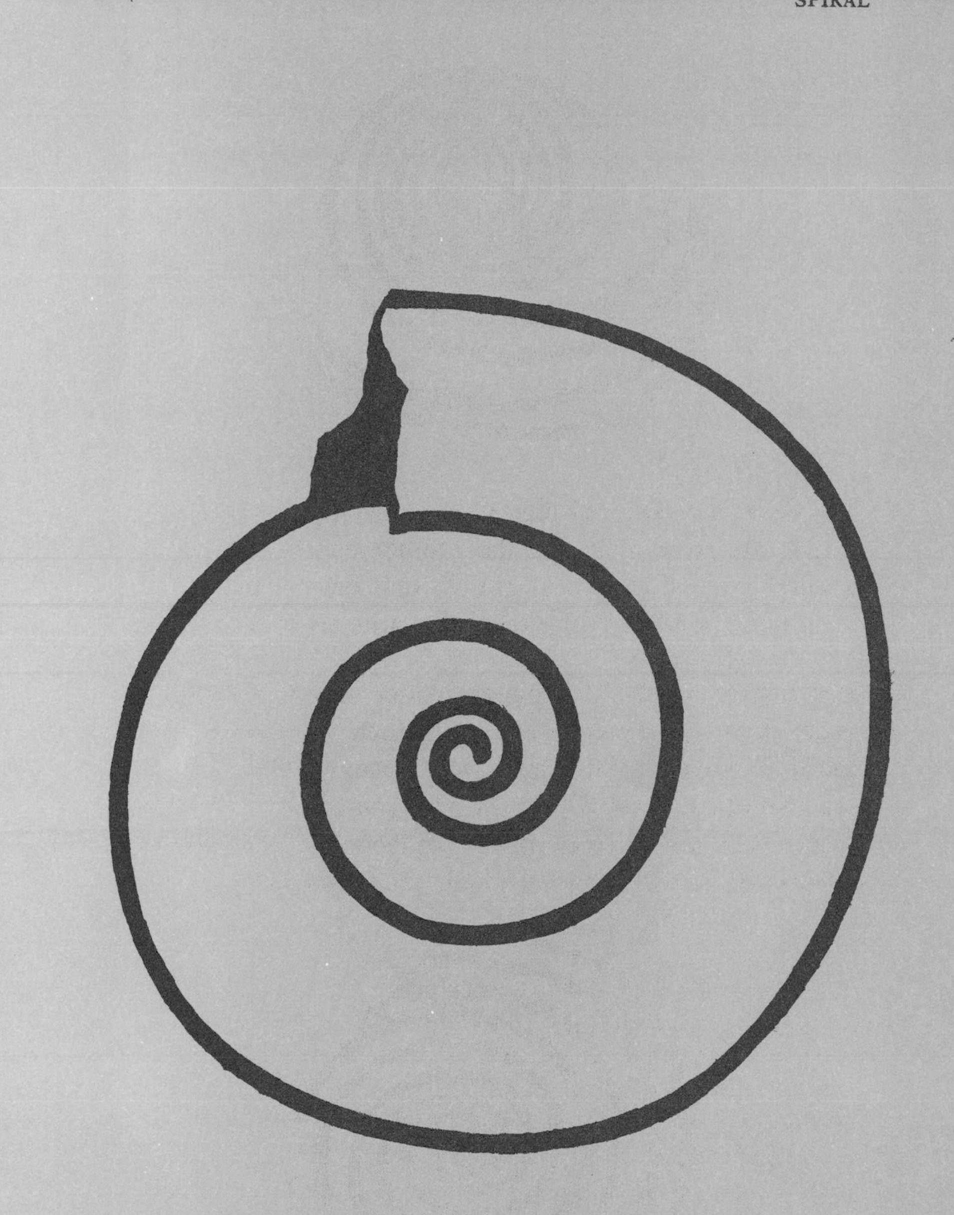

On the seed heads of sunflowers and daisies and at the bases of fir cones you will find a fascinating pattern of interlocking spirals. This pattern can be drawn on a piece of paper, 6 inches by 6 inches, if you take some care.

1. Join the midpoints of the sides of the square.
2. Mark points 1¼ inches from each corner. Join each one to the center.
3. Divide one of the lines into ¼ inch parts.
4. Draw a circle through each one of the divisions.
5. Connect points as shown.
6. Then draw a spiral going the other way.

If you are really ambitious you can draw more of the design by putting in all twelve possible spirals in the figure. It will give you more of the picture of the pattern on the seed heads.

The spirals you see in the hairspring of a watch or on a phonograph record are made in a different way. You can make one like it with a pencil and paper, some thread and a nail. Wrap the thread around the nail and tie a loop for your pencil point. Pound the nail into a flat piece of soft wood under your paper. As the thread unwinds it will guide your pencil in a spiral.

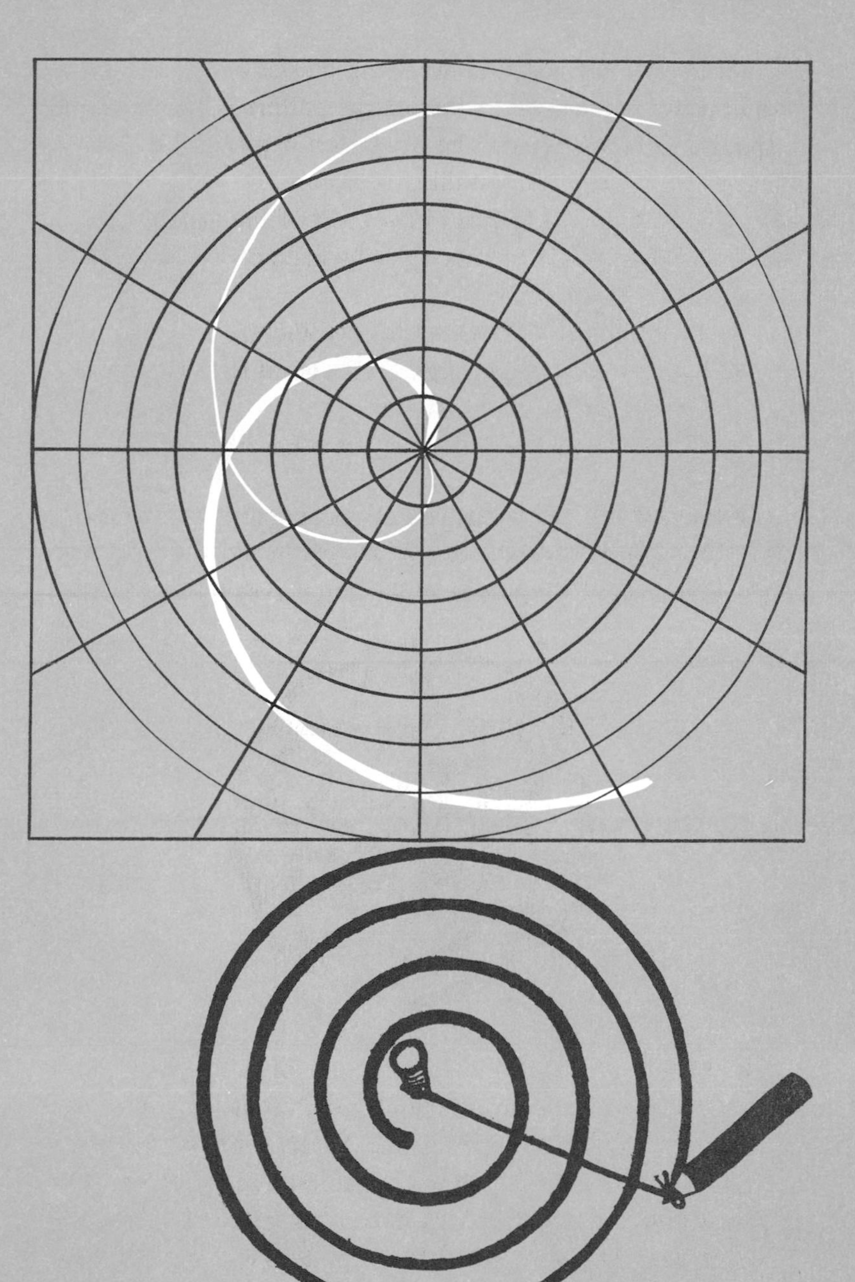

Another kind of spiral is found on bolts and screws, on a barber pole, and as part of a spiral staircase. This kind of spiral is called a **helix**.

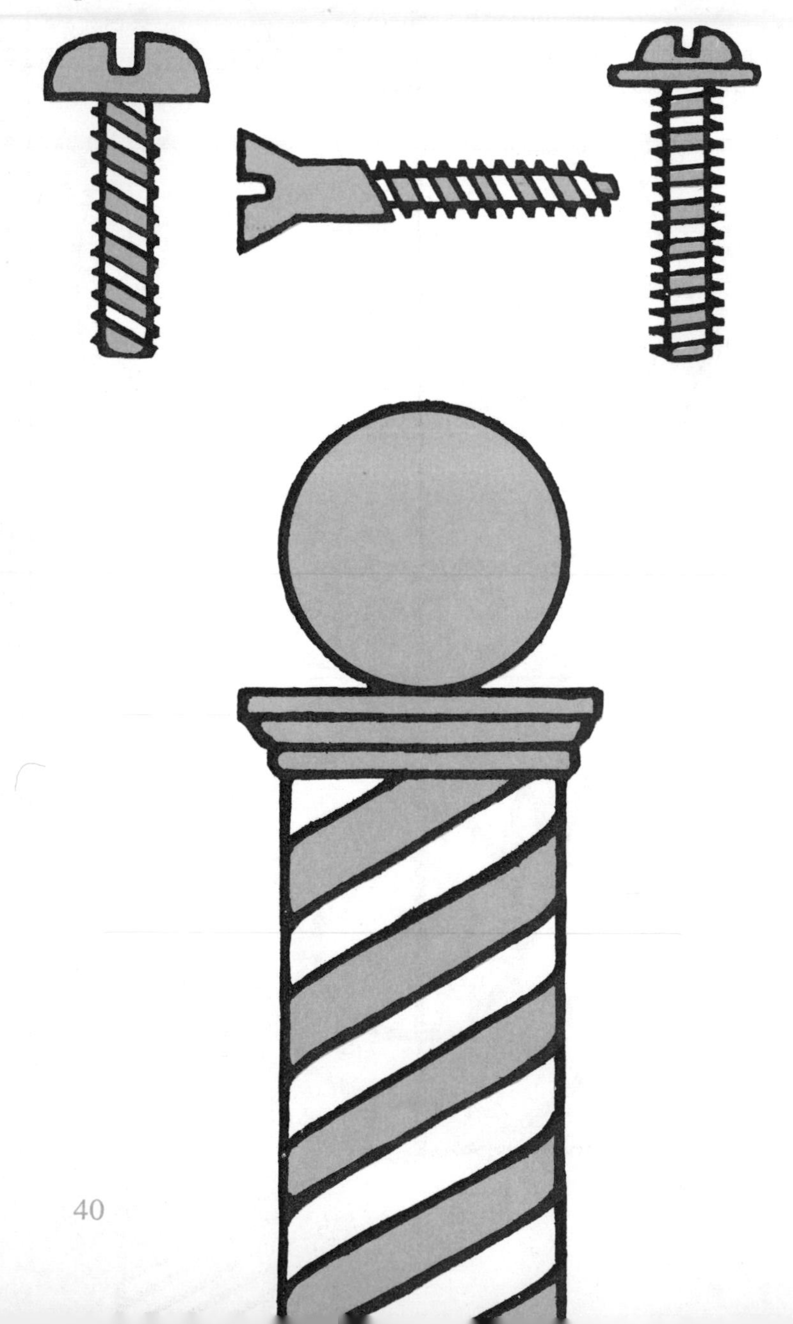

So far in this book we have mainly looked at shapes that have two dimensions. The mathematician calls these shapes **plane figures**. He sees them in his mind as having no thickness at all. When a figure has three dimensions, the mathematician calls it a **space figure**.

The first space figure we will look at is called a **cylinder**. This comes from a Greek word meaning "a roll." A cylinder is formed when a circle gains thickness or height.

A penny is in the shape of a cylinder.

A pile of pennies makes us think of a taller cylinder.

With a strip of paper 10 inches long and 2 inches wide you can make a helix. With a thick colored line, join the upper left-hand corner to the lower right-hand corner. Cut through the middle of this line with a scissors. Take one of these pieces and roll it from the wide end around a pencil as shown. The helix will appear as a colored line.

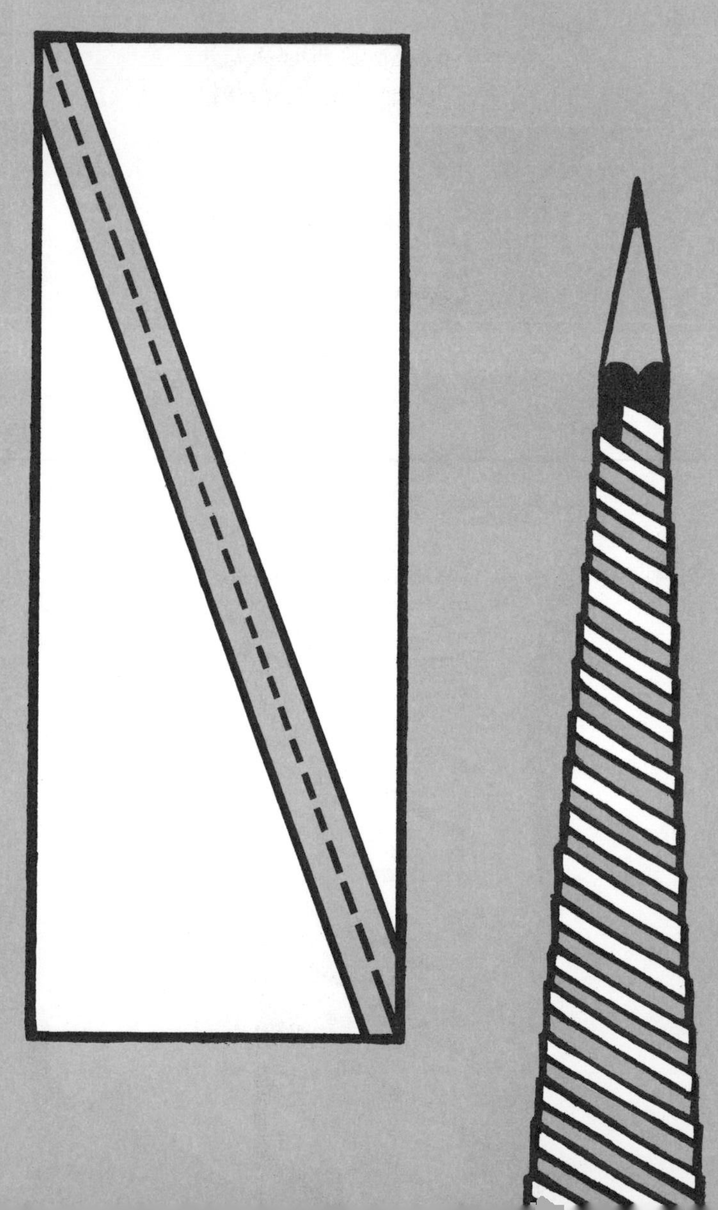

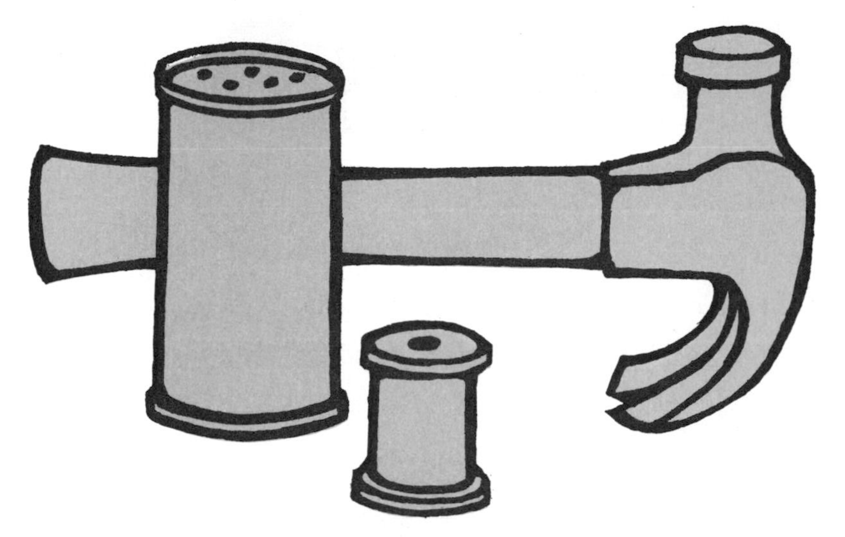

Make a collection of the names of as many things as you can that have a cylinder as their basic shape. Try to find a reason for the choice of this shape in each case.

For instance, coins are usually cylindrical so that the wear caused by their rubbing together is the same all around. If they were square the corners would wear first.

Most pens and pencils, and some handles, are cylinders because this shape fits the hand well when you grip it. Wind a long length of string around the center part of a square-shaped piece of wood. From the shape the string rolls into, you will soon see why most spools and wheels are cylindrical.

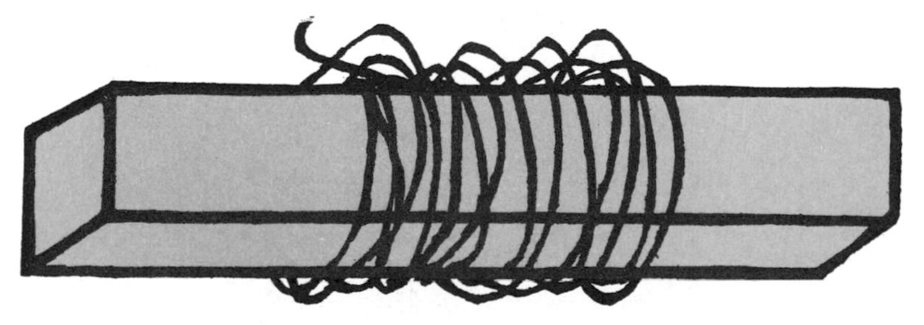

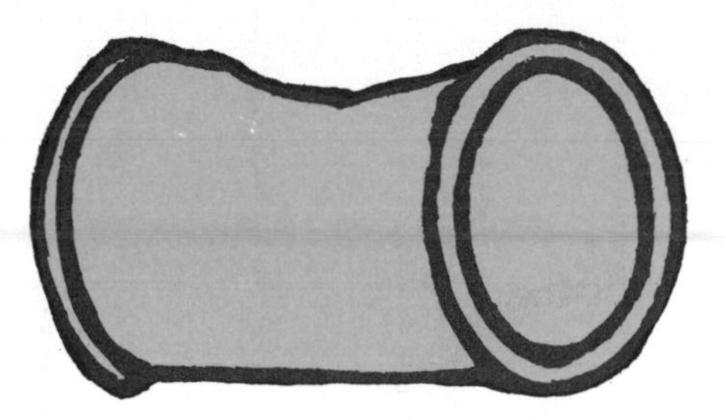

Some cylinders in your collection will be the sort that contain substances under pressure such as an Aerosol can or the boiler of a locomotive.

You may wonder why the cylinder shape was chosen. To find out, take a cylindrical can and lay it on its side on a hard surface. Also take a rectangularly shaped can made from the same kind of metal and place it on the same hard surface. Try to crush each can with your foot and notice which needs the most pressure before it begins to buckle.

This is one reason why the cans for most foods are cylindrical. Canned foods must be sealed and cooked under high-pressure steam, and a square or rectangular can might bend. Also important is the fact that the cylinder is an economical shape to make from a given amount of tin. It will contain more food than other kinds of cans made from the same amount of material. Think about your Gold Claim and you will see why.

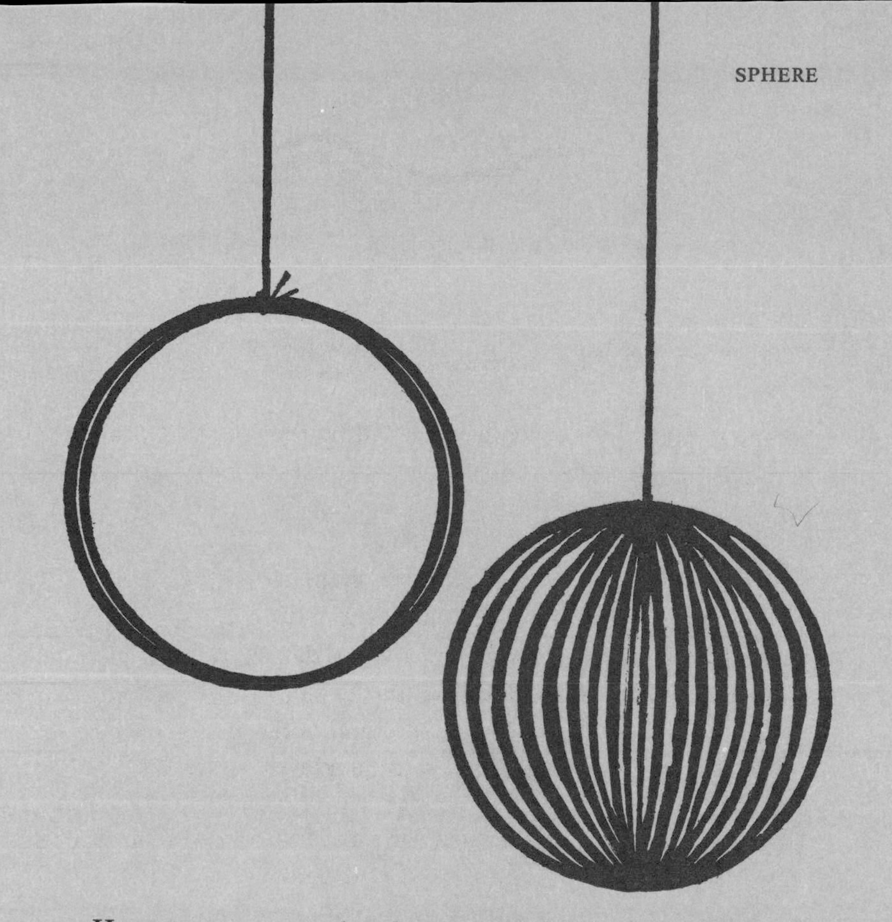

Have you ever wondered why some castles have towers of different shapes in their walls? Often square towers were built first, but it was found that cannon balls easily damaged their corners. Wise owners then rebuilt them in a cylindrical shape so that the cannon balls would be more likely to bounce off.

If we hang a hoop by a string and spin it around like this, then it will trace out the surface of a space figure that makes us think of a ball. The mathematician calls this shape a **sphere**, but we were not far wrong since "sphere" comes from a Greek word meaning "a ball." The sphere is the perfect space figure. Nature shows us some of its properties.

Bubble blowing is an old game, and the shape of the bubbles shows us that the sphere is nature's choice to contain the most air for the least amount of surface area. This is true whether the bubbles are in air or in a liquid.

What shape does a rectangular paper bag try to take as you blow it up before bursting it? Much of the skill of the glass blower depends upon this choice, which nature has made.

A sphere is the shape that will enclose the most space using the smallest possible surface. We have seen that nature knows this, and man has copied this idea. We like many liquids we drink to be hot. When hot things come into contact with the air they cool. We often find that containers of hot liquids have a sphere as their basic shape, for in this way we can have the greatest amount of liquid for the least amount of cooling surface. Think about a teapot.

The shape is the basic shape of the many sizes and kinds of balls used in games. Different sports require balls made of varying materials, but most are made in spherical shape. But at least one game has varied the shape. What game uses a ball shaped like this?

You may not see all these yourself, so keep your eyes open for examples in pictures, films, and on television. If you have a camera of your own, perhaps you could start a collection of curves that you have seen. The camera lens itself is, of course, a curved shape.

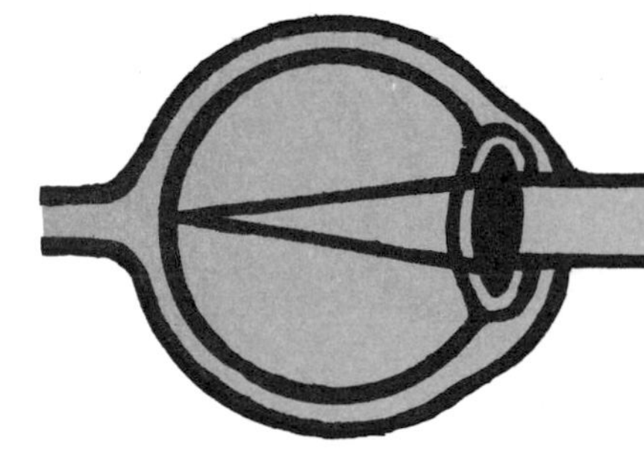

We use lenses to explore the tiniest details of our world and through lenses we also look out into space. But without the curved shapes that are the lenses of our own eyes we could see none of these things–and you could not have read this book.

There has not been enough space in this book to mention all the curves that exist. Perhaps by now you have realized that curves can be seen in many places; in bridges, in domes, in arches, in musical instruments, and in churches.

ARTHUR RAZZELL and K. G. O. WATTS are two Englishmen, presently living in London and teaching education in schools there. Mr. Razzell, born in Kent, was married after serving in the Second World War and has three children—two boys and a girl. Mr. Watts served as a radar mechanic in the Royal Air Force. Originally from Hampshire, he is married and has two young children.

ELLEN RASKIN was born in Milwaukee, Wisconsin, and lived there until she went to the University of Wisconsin. While still in college, she decided on art as a career, and she has been extraordinarily successful. Miss Raskin has illustrated many children's books and has done over 900 book jackets, plus magazine and advertising illustrations. She now lives in New York City.

DONALD H. FIRL, the Educational Consultant to the EXPLORING MATHEMATICS series, is the mathematics consultant for the Rochester, Minnesota, public schools. A graduate of Gustavus Adolphus College and Kansas State University of Iowa, and Carleton College. Mr. Firl has been an author of a mathematics series published by the National Council of Teachers of Mathematics, as well as a children's Christmas play. In addition to supervising the mathematics instruction of all children from kindergarten through high school in Rochester, he has five children of his own.